WRITE HUMOR!
LEARN HOW TO PRODUCE FUNNY MATERIAL ON A REGULAR SCHEDULE

CHANDRA CLARKE

OBSIDIAN OWL
PRESS

Write Humor! Learn How to Produce Funny Material on a Regular Schedule

© Chandra K. Clarke 1997-2023.

This book was originally released under the title *Humor Writing – The Art of Being Funny*. This version has been revised and updated.

All rights reserved. Without limiting the rights under the copyright reserved above, no part of this publication may be reproduced, stored in, or introduced into a retrieval system, or transmitted in any form or by any means (electronic, mechanical, photocopying, recording, or otherwise) without prior written permission.

While every effort has been made to ensure the accuracy and legitimacy of the references, referrals, and links (collectively "Links") presented in this book, the author is not responsible or liable for broken Links or missing or fallacious information at the Links. Any Links in this book to a specific product, process, web site, or service do not constitute or imply an endorsement by the author of same, or its producer or provider. The views and opinions contained at any Links do not necessarily express or reflect those of the author.

Although the author and publisher have made every effort to ensure that the information in this book was correct at press time, the author and publisher do not assume and hereby disclaim any liability to any party for any loss, damage, or disruption caused by errors or omissions, whether such errors or omissions result from negligence, accident, or any other cause.

Paperback ISBN: 978-1-7772174-4-0

Ebook ISBN: 978-1-7772174-5-7

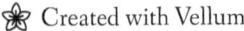 Created with Vellum

BEFORE WE BEGIN

This book consists of six chapters designed to get you thinking critically about humor — what it is, what it's for, how to use it — so you can write with it. More than that, you'll be able to write humor on a regular schedule, rather than just waiting for the muse to wander by.

The material here will be of use to the writer looking to become a full-fledged humorist, as well as to those of you who want to add zing to your style generally. Basically, I hope to teach you how to sharpen your wit. And if you've lost your wit along with the change under the sofa cushions, or aren't sure you had one to begin with, well, this course should help you with that, too.

I'd suggest going through one chapter per week so that you complete the whole book in six weeks. You can take more or less time than that if you want, but the lessons were designed to be completed on a one-per-week basis.

Right, enough of that. Before we get started, the obligatory:[1]

WHO AM I?

I have no idea who you are. Perhaps we could sit down with a virtual cup of coffee and...

NO, I MEAN WHO ARE YOU? WHY SHOULD I LISTEN TO YOU?

Ohhh, I see. I'm Chandra Clarke. I have written for publications like *Popular Science*, *Canadian Business*, and yes, *Voice of the Kent Farmer*. I write a popular online blog, and my most recent book, *Pundragon*, has been compared (favorably!) to the work of Sir Terry Pratchett and Douglas Adams. If you like credentials, I have a PhD in creative writing. Yes, that's a thing.

---

1. Unless otherwise noted, the examples from blog posts are my own.

CHAPTER ONE

THE ART OF BEING FUNNY

When I went through university, I noticed that every introductory textbook I ever had started out with a cornball definition section such as: "What is cultural anthropology? (anthro-POL-ogee)" or "What is thermonuclear physics? (FIZZicks)" Naturally, I couldn't resist such an opening here. Sooooo [ahem]:

WHAT IS HUMOR?

At this point, textbook authors usually retreat to the dictionary which, in our case, would say something like: "something which arouses amusement, laughter etc.; the capacity for recognizing, reacting to, or expressing something which is amusing; a mood, frame of mind, in a good humor, in no humor to be contradicted."

There's more, of course, but I didn't think you and Webster wanted to be that well acquainted. Besides which, in typical dictionary fashion, this definition has cross-referenced us to other things that need definitions, like: What the heck is amusement anyway? We'll handle that later. For now, here's another definition of humor that's far more useful to our purposes:

"Humour may be defined as the kindly contemplation of the incongruities of life and the artistic expression thereof."

Who said this? A humorist by the name of Stephen Leacock, which is why this definition is more useful than anything a dictionary had to say. (Leacock was Canadian, incidentally, like me, hence the spelling of "humour.") He's telling us that humor is a way of looking at daily life, spotting the boo-boos, and pointing them out in a way that cracks people up.

But, why bother? Why not just point things out in a straightforward manner and say, "Yo! We done screwed up here!" Why do we go through all the trouble of trying to make people laugh?

Believe it or not, there are entire textbooks that ask that very same question. People study the psychology of humor and try to come up with theories as to why it's necessary and why humans are so keen on it. I'll summarize the major types of theories below.

(Attention: This is the bit you can repeat to your friends at your next swanky cocktail party. Rather than saying, "Yeah, I took this course called Chuckles 101," you can say, "Yes, really dahling, well, when I studied the theoretical perspectives and empirical issues in the psychology of humor, the major schools of thought were...." A word of warning, though: It's best not to attempt to say words like "theoretical perspectives" after your third cocktail.)

THEORIES OF HUMOR

Biological - Folks who support the biological-type theories say that laughter and humor do nice things like restore homeostasis, stabilize blood pressure, oxygenate the blood, massage the vital organs, stimulate circulation, facilitate digestion and relax the system. In other words: Duh, we laugh because it feels good.

Instinct - Other theorists think that we use laughter as a defense mechanism against things that are depressing or disagreeable. For instance, if our cavemen ancestors hadn't found a way to deal with the sight of Mr. Argh E. Ugh being flattened by a woolly mammoth, the species would have been too depressed and scared to go on.

Evolution - There are a bunch of different perspectives lumped under this heading. Some suggest that laughter served as a communication function in the days before language. It signaled good news and that it was safe to relax, or perhaps social laughter expressed unity in group opinion. Other researchers suggest that laughter is a relic of struggling, biting and physical attack, pointing out the similarities between baring your teeth and smiling. They presume that gradually laughter and humor became a substitute for actual assault. Considering the biting commentary of some late-night talk show hosts, this might not be far off....

Superiority - Proponents of superiority theories think that the roots of laughter lie in triumph over other people. We feel good when we compare ourselves favorably to others who we feel are stupid, ugly, less fortunate or weak. According to these folks, mockery, ridicule and laughter at the expense of other people are central to humor. This could be dubbed the "nyah nyah" school of thought.

Incongruity - This theory, which harkens back to Leacock's definition of humor, suggests that humor comes from pairing mismatched ideas or contradictory concepts. We find the square peg trying to fit into the round hole funny. This could also be called the oxymoron theory of humor, e.g., political integrity or military intelligence.

Surprise - Elements of surprise, shock, and suddenness are thought to be important aspects of humor. In other words, we laugh because we weren't expecting the outcome. This goes a long way to explaining why people have found the old "slip on a banana peel" gag funny: We are surprised, at least the first time, at the pratfall. It also explains why, to most people, jokes aren't as funny the second or third time through.

Release and Relief - These theories say that we use humor to relieve stress and tension, as well as to dissipate excess energy. Although toddlers are not known to have high stress levels, they do have tons of energy, so this theory might be good for explaining why little kids giggle so much. It also explains why you tend to dissolve into hysterical laughter after spending four hours to get your printer to spit out a two-page report.

Configurational - This theory contends that humor is experienced when two things that are originally thought to be unrelated suddenly fall into place. This is the opposite of incongruity: In that theory, we find humor in disjointed relationships, but this theory proposes that we find humor in discovering relationships we didn't know existed. This is otherwise known as the "Hey! I never thought of that!" theory.[1]

ENOUGH THEORIZING, ALREADY!

Okay, so now we've reviewed what the academics have come up with. Which of these theories is the right one? Well, if you're anything like me, when you read them, you found elements of truth in all of them. Who hasn't heard — and yes, laughed at — a joke that makes fun of someone else? Who hasn't felt better after a good, long laugh? So, as with most psychological theories, the answer is that all of them are right in varying degrees, depending on the situation. Humans are complex critters, and no one theory or answer is going to cover all the bases.

Now that we've done our research, we're a bit better equipped to answer the question posed by that dictionary definition: What do we find amusing or...

WHAT'S SO FUNNY?

Obviously, we find things funny when they make us feel better physically and mentally, when they surprise us, and when they show us things in a different light. Sounds all very neat and simple now, doesn't it? Well, if it was all that easy to figure out, I'd be out of a job! So, here's the problem: Different people get these feelings from different things.

For instance, some people find the sight and sound of someone burping to be absolutely hilarious. Others prefer biting satire and political comedy. Your neighbor might love the comedy routines of Buster Keaton or the Three Stooges. Your Aunt Griselda, meanwhile, laughs herself silly at improv. Personally (although they're often referred to as the lowest form of humor), I love puns. Furthermore, I believe that a truly good pun should hurt.

Let's get a bit more specific and examine the different forms that humor and comedy take.

TYPES OF HUMOR

Here's a completely unscientific, but mostly organized look at some of the different types of humor.

Bathroom/Scatological Humor - This is the category that burping falls under. Generally, this type consists of actual bodily functions (flatulence, sexual responses, etc.) at inappropriate moments, or jokes about the same. It depends mainly on shock or surprise value, and it helps us to laugh at and make fun of the establishment.

Pratfalls - Slips, trips, tumbles and falls. This very physical comedy occurs when someone does something that would normally hurt, maim or kill — yet, somehow the character always manages to get up and walk away. Popular in cartoons, it was also a feature in shows like *Three's Company* and *Home Alone*. It is another type of humor that depends on shock and surprise, as well as the superiority aspect, as we like to laugh at people who are dumb enough to let themselves get into such situations.

Sight Gags - This type of comedy usually runs in the background or in parallel with other action. It can take many forms: physical comedy (someone getting clobbered in the distance), jokes on signs hanging on a wall, visual puns and so on. The Leslie Neilson *Police Squad* series and *The Simpsons* use sight gags. Sight gags are different because, for the most part, writers don't call attention to the jokes, so half the fun for the audience is watching for them, while also keeping track of the main action.

One-liners/Quips - One or two sentences that contain both the setup and the punchline in a neat, compact package. Stand-up comedians use a lot of one-liners, as do sitcoms, bumper stickers, greeting cards and even Internet memes. One-liners can work by taking a common cliché/phrase/lyric and changing it (e.g., "people who live in glass houses shouldn't" or "I owe, I owe, so it's off to work I go"), by swiftly summing up tensions or frustrations

("How do you make a computer go faster? Throw it harder."), or by briefly illuminating an incongruity or configuration ("Communism is the equal distribution of poverty").

Burlesque - This is all about taking an ordinary situation to the extreme. Three examples come to mind here: a Monty Python skit involving two fighting knights in armor who dismember each other completely yet keep fighting; a *Saturday Night Live* skit where an airline steward obsequiously says "buh-bye" to all his passengers as they disembark in mid-air; and finally, an *I Love Lucy* scene where she's working on a candy manufacturing conveyor belt gone mad. She ends up stuffing candies into her mouth, down her blouse and so forth in a vain attempt to keep on top of the situation.

Plain Old Jokes - You know what I mean: knock-knocks, riddles, question/answer routines. These usually have common formats like the tried and true, "Why is an X like a Y?" (e.g., Q: Why is a cat like a gossip? A: They are both tale bearers.), the ever-popular lightbulb joke (e.g., Q: How many junkies does it take to change a lightbulb? A: Wow, is it like, dark, man? or Q: How many editors does it take to change a lightbulb? A: Two, one to change the bulb and one to issue a rejection letter to the old bulb.), and let's not forget the priest, rabbi and minister in a bar format (e.g., A priest, a minister and a rabbi walk into a bar. The bartender says, "Hey! Is this some kind of joke?").

Anecdotes - These are mildly funny short stories, usually designed to make a point about human behavior or illustrate an aspect of life. Anecdotes can be found in places like *Reader's Digest* or heard around the water cooler at work. Here's an example you have probably seen on the Internet:

At a busy airport, a crowded flight was cancelled. A single agent was rebooking a long line of inconvenienced travelers. Suddenly, an angry passenger pushed his way to the desk.

He slapped his ticket down on the counter and said, "I HAVE to be on this flight, and it has to be first class."

The agent replied, "I'm sorry, sir. I'll be happy to try to help you, but I've got to help these folks first, and I'm sure we'll be able to work something out. Please get back in line."

The passenger was unimpressed. He asked loudly, so that the passengers behind him could hear, "Do you have any idea who I am?"

Without hesitating, the gate agent smiled and grabbed her public address microphone. "May I have your attention please?" she began, her voice bellowing throughout the terminal. "We have a passenger here at the gate WHO DOES NOT KNOW WHO HE IS. If anyone can help him find his identity, please come to the gate."

With the folks behind him in line laughing, the man glared at the agent, gritted his teeth and swore, saying, "F* you."

Without flinching, she smiled and said, "I'm sorry, sir, but you'll have to stand in line for that, too."

The man retreated as the people in the terminal applauded loudly. Although the flight was canceled and people were late, they were no longer angry at the airline.

Parodies - In this form of humor, you imitate something to make fun of it. Usually, the target is something well-known — political figures, popular songs, movies, TV shows. Many *Saturday Night Live* skits do this, and "Weird Al" Yankovic has made a good living making fun of pop songs like Madonna's "Like a Virgin" (which he changed to "Like a Surgeon"). The movie *Galaxy Quest* was a great parody of the *Star Trek* series.

Satire - This type of humor pokes fun at something by stressing or exaggerating its worst features. Editorial cartoonists use satire frequently, usually related to politics and governmental affairs. *The Simpsons* also uses satire often, as do *Mad Magazine* and *Cracked* and the *National Lampoon* movies (starring Chevy Chase).

Limericks & Light Verse - Although you don't often see them used these days, limericks, verses and rhymes are another form of humorous expression. Edward Lear is probably the most famous author of limericks, many of which he wrote for children:

There was an Old Person whose habits

Induced him to feed upon Rabbits.

When he'd eaten eighteen, he turned perfectly green,

Upon which he relinquished those habits.

There's also the famous Nantucket limericks.[2] This series of limericks was discovered in a June 14, 1924 edition of a Nantucket newspaper. It all began when *The Princeton Tiger* revived the then well-known limerick printed below and *The Chicago Tribune* answered with the second limerick. *The New York Exchange* went one step further with the third rhyme, and *The Pawtucket Times* took over from there:

There once was a man from Nantucket,

Who kept all of his cash in a bucket,

But his daughter, named Nan,

Ran away with a man.

And as for the bucket, Nantucket.

— *The Princeton Tiger*

But he followed the pair to Pawtucket,

The man and the girl with the bucket:

And he said to the man.

He was welcome to Nan.

But as for the bucket, Pawtucket.

— *The Chicago Tribune*

Then the pair followed Pa to Manhasset,

Where he still held the cash as an asset,

But Nan and the man

Stole the money and ran.

And as for the bucket, Manhasset.

— *The New York Exchange*

Of this story we hear from Nantucket.

About the mysterious loss of a bucket.

We are sorry for Nan.

As well as the man-

The cash and the bucket. Pawtucket.

— The *Pawtucket Times*

And so on, and so on....

Dark Humor - This type of humor deals with dark subjects like death, war, disease, broken relationships, all that hilarious stuff. It probably most typifies the instinct theory — laughing at things that bother us in order to deal with them. Two movies that are examples of this kind of comedy are *War of the Roses* and, to a lesser degree, *Weekend at Bernie's*.

Funny Characters - Sometimes movies, TV shows, books and magazines will have a serious intent generally, but use funny characters to lighten the tone or provide comic relief. The neurotic character Greg Medavoy often eases dramatic tension on *NYPD Blue*, which deals with topics like murder, sexual assault and cancer. Disney cartoons almost always have one zany creature that delights both adults and children, like the meerkat in *The Lion King* or the raccoon in *Pocahontas*. Humor is also used to make characters more likeable and more human.

For example, Diana Gabaldon's *Outlander* series (historical romance) makes for a good read because, A) it is set in Scotland, which always fascinates; B) it's a romance, and we know what aspect of that sells; and C) her characters have a great sense of humor. The reader can relate across time and space to her 1700s Scottish hero Jamie because he laughs — at himself and at life. Which brings me to...

WHY BE FUNNY?

A basic question, but an important one nevertheless. It's something you should ask yourself before we get into the nitty gritty of actually learning how to be funny. You see, it all has to do with motivation.

Most people want to be funny because, well, people like you better. It's true! The life of the party is the one cracking jokes and making people laugh. If you know how to make people laugh, then more often than not, you'll be the center of attention. Furthermore, there's money in them thar belly laughs: sitcoms, comic strips, editorial cartoons, magazines, movies, bumper stickers. Humor sells.

But, the kicker here is: So do a lot of other things — sex, for one. So, why do you want to write humor instead of erotica? What is it you want to accomplish with humor?

Personally, I have two reasons for writing humor. First, I love to make people laugh — not just because it helps me win friends and influence people, although that's certainly a factor. More importantly, I like to make people feel good. I like the sound of laughter, and I like the way people's faces light up when they hear or read something funny. The world is full of doom and gloom and dark stuff. I like waving my little flashlight about whenever I can.

Second, I love to make people think. Humor is a great way to point out inconsistencies, present new ideas and suggest improvements in a non-threatening way. Humor takes the sting out of criticism and reduces the tensions involved in contemplating the unknown.

The TV show *All in the Family* poked fun at many stereotypes by representing them with comical characters. If the writers on that show had come out and said, "America, some of your most cherished beliefs are stupid, outmoded and intolerant — especially you there, yeah, you in the red shirt in the front row!" they probably would have just made everyone mad, particularly Mr. Red Shirt. Even worse, the beliefs they were talking about would become more firmly entrenched because humans are basically contrary creatures and tend to get defensive. However, by personifying those same ideals in the less-than-bright Archie and the ditzy Edith, and then mocking them, the same point is made, but in a far more acceptable way. As Will Rogers once said, "Anything is funny if it happens to another person."

So, to get back to the question, you have to ask yourself: What is my motivation to write humor? Money, entertainment, education, self-fulfillment? All of the above? The answers are important because it's hard to write without a purpose in mind. Your purpose tends to shape your approach to the craft.

WILL THIS CHAPTER NEVER END?

Yep. Just did, in fact. Now we get to the fun — your "homework assignment."

Your mission, should you choose to accept it, is to determine the answers to the following questions:

1. I'll bet in reading through the different types of humor, you said to yourself, "Hey! What kind of a writer is this? She missed X and Y!" What other types of humor can you think of, and can you provide well-known examples?
2. Over the next week, when you are reading, listening to the radio or watching TV, take note of what makes you laugh. Then figure out *why* it made you laugh.

3. Over the next week, when you are reading, listening to the radio, or watching TV, take note of what makes you laugh out loud. What? Didn't I just ask that question? Not quite. If you think about it, you will often laugh to yourself when you come across something funny, or perhaps you just allowed for a smile. When something is really funny, though, you'll laugh out loud. Since the "LOL" is what every humor writer strives for, it's an important distinction. Figure out why it made you cut loose when other things didn't.

While you're at it, observe what makes *other* people laugh to themselves and what makes them laugh out loud. This is even more important than 2) and 3) because, while laughing at your own jokes makes for a happy existence, it doesn't pay the bills. Try to figure out (either by observation or direct questioning) why they laughed — or didn't. (BIG HINT: Do not preface any question with: "Why the heck did you think that was funny? That was stupid! What are you, some kind of moron?" The idea is to find out what makes people tick, not to tick them off!)

---

1. For more on such theories see: http://www.slate.com/blogs/browbeat/2011/05/13/5_leading_theories_for_why_we_laugh_and_the_jokes_that_prove_them_wrong.html, and https://en.wikipedia.org/wiki/Theories_of_humor
2. https://en.wikipedia.org/wiki/There_once_was_a_man_from_Nantucket

CHAPTER TWO

WHERE TO FIND IDEAS

What? Back for more? A real glutton for punishment, aren't you? Okay, if you insist....

Probably the most common question I get on my blog is: "Where do you come up with this stuff?" Normally, I just claim to have a direct pipeline to divine sources of creativity because who wants to ruin the writer's mystique? But, since you're one of us (you did supply the password at the front gate, didn't you?), I'll be a little more specific.

INGEST HUMOR REGULARLY

That may sound obvious, but you'd be amazed at how many people forget this step. If you're a literary fiction writer, the best way to stimulate your mind is to read the works of other literary fiction authors on a regular basis. If you're into science fiction, then read the works of other sci-fi creators. Likewise, if you want to write humor, read the work of other funny writers. Listen to funny radio shows and watch funny stuff on TV and at the theatre.

I'm not talking about sitting there and analyzing a work — we'll discuss that later under writing techniques. I'm talking about getting yourself into the right frame of mind for writing humor.

Relax. Enjoy. Absorb.

Why? If you read nothing but news magazines and watch nothing but teary-eyed movies-of-the- week, chances are that you will unconsciously pick up the style and flow of that material and will be applying that to your own work. It will be even worse if the majority of your writing income currently comes from writing something other than humor. It's very difficult to switch gears.

So, make sure you make humor part of your daily life. If you're going to be as porous as a sponge, you might as well soak up a little of what you want to produce. Be sure to sample widely. Even if you're not fond of stand-up, for example, check out a show occasionally to see what's hot. Read long pieces like books and short pieces like columns and one-liners. Take in the works of both women and men — because at least half your audience is not the same gender to you!

And don't forget to reach across space and time for material. The American sense of humor is quite different than the Canadian sense, which is different again than the

British — and all are vastly different from the Chinese sense of humor. Shop around; examine different cultures.

Head to your local library to check out past masters to find out what styles and subjects made people laugh through the ages. Thumb through the works of the ancient Celts, skim something by a few notable old Greeks, research how they chuckled in the Dark Ages (the peasants may have been revolting, but the humorists were good), slide on through the Renaissance to find out why *Mona Lisa* was smiling and so on.

It also helps to read one or two short pieces immediately before you begin your own work, just to prime the pump. Having said that, of course, I'm now going to say...

READ OTHER TYPES OF MATERIAL

Yes, I know, I know. I just got through telling you to consume humor, and now I'm telling you to read other stuff.

Ingesting humor is good for putting you in the right frame of mind (i.e., a warped one), and that's important. However, if you go about taking in nothing but funny stuff, you run the risk of becoming stale. Too much of anything isn't a good idea. The brain, like the body, needs a well-balanced diet. Plus, if you seem to do nothing but laugh hysterically while you're consuming media, your family will have to consider putting in a call to the local psychiatric ward.

Reading other genres will help you learn more about the craft of writing. A particularly well-turned phrase, vivid imagery, crackling dialogue — all of it will help you grow as a writer. A joke won't work if you step all over it with clumsy phrasing, and you need to know how to fill in the bits around the punchlines.

In addition, it is from this material that you will get your ideas. This is the stuff you use to...

BUILD A HUMOR FILE

When you read a newspaper or hear the local broadcast, chances are you'll find something that piques your interest. Perhaps it will be an item about a dumb criminal who got caught in mid-robbery, or a new government initiative that sounds worrisome. Most days you probably just shrug it off in favor of thinking of your grocery list or your upcoming credit card bill.

Hey, you're a humor writer now. It's time to start taking notes!

From now on, clip out or scribble down anything you come across that arouses an emotion — be it anger, fear, annoyance, sadness or laughter. Carry a small notepad, a pen and a pencil (because pens inevitably run out of ink at the worst possible moment) in the car or in your purse to jot down notes. If it provokes a reaction in you, it will likely provoke a reaction in other people, too — and therefore it's fodder for a humor piece.

(BIG HINT: Do not take the scissors to the newspapers or magazines in your house, if you still get paper copies, unless everyone has read them already. No matter how hilarious your finished product is, your relatives will *not* be amused at your Swiss cheese approach to inspiration.)

(ANOTHER BIG HINT: If you keep a notepad in the car, do not attempt to scribble things while changing lanes, merging with a major freeway, parallel parking or when the engine is running. To do otherwise is known as the Swiss cheese approach to driving and tends to leave bits of you and your automobile on the road.)

Your clippings file can consist of things like advertisements, comic strips, police reports, statistics, business news, entertainment tidbits, good quotes, punchlines, editorials, headlines, jokes, advice, sports — whatever catches your eye. Good apps for this include Pocket (for saving URLs), and Evernote (for saving URLs, images, notes, etc). As of this writing I also still use an RSS reader to subscribe to a variety of blogs and sites I follow; I also use Blendle to read individual articles from paid subscription publications. Apple News is another alternative that appears to be an all you can read monthly subscription model. Oh, and while I'm at it, I do my searches with Ecosia. Every time you do a search, their ad revenue goes into planting trees, at no cost to you.

Speaking of eyes and ears, keep them wide open as you go about your daily business. Pay attention to what your coworkers complain about at the water cooler. Take down details of the four-year-old's wrestling match with the grocery cart at the store. Whenever you're waiting in line, listen to how people talk and what they talk about. Snippets of conversation are great inspiration and provide good examples of real dialogue.

ER, BUT ISN'T THIS ALSO CALLED COPYRIGHT INFRINGEMENT AND EAVESDROPPING?

Nonononol! I don't mean for you to steal lines, jokes or stories, or to hover over other restaurant patrons with a notebook in hand. This is not a good way to win friends (and you may find yourself the lucky recipient of a black eye). But good jokes, clever quotes and oddball stories will provide you with the foundations for building your own material.

For example, if you recall in Chapter One, I mentioned a line that went, "People who live in glass houses shouldn't." That line is a twist on the phrase, "People who live in glass houses shouldn't throw stones." The latter phrase has been around for years, but one day somebody looked at it with that slightly warped perspective of the humor writer, and gave it a kick. What fresh approach can you use on this line or other one-line bits of advice?

Here's another example: A while ago, I came across a piece in the paper about a cargo ship that had lost several containers of Lego toys at sea. The article went on to mention other spills, including one of Nike shoes, another of candy, and it talked about how the contents of these containers wash up on shore in faraway places. To me, it screamed out BLOG POST, and eventually I worked it into a piece involving a wounded octopus, several bad fish puns, hockey and a serious point about environmental pollution. Really.

"Uh-huh," you're saying to yourself, "so you lucked out with a Lego article that screamed at you. Bet you're one of those people who has a talking washing machine, too, just like on TV. What are the rest of us supposed to do?"

Well, says I, anticipating this question, remember what I said about things provoking a reaction? If the item caught your attention in the first place and then went on to hold your attention, it's a potential target. If it arouses an emotion within you, especially a strong one, it's definitely a target.

More specifically, places to find ideas can include:

Magazine Articles/Listicles - You've seen those features. "Ten tips to make yourself beautiful!" or "Men! Things your wife wants you to know but won't tell you!" These are great sources for parody.

The Shared Experience - The commonality of life in the modern Western world means that we share a lot of experiences — and a lot of frustrations. The comic strip *Dilbert* feeds off the frustration of the average office worker dealing with corporate existence. Most of us go grocery shopping, take our kids to the hockey rink or little league and fight the dandelions in our lawns. What's your take on these situations? Incidentally, the shared experience — if handled well — will probably generate the most reader feedback. This is because people like laughing over those incongruities, and they really like recognizing some aspect of their own lives in your work.

There is nothing quite as satisfying as finding out there are others out there with a cranky boss, bad restaurant service, an ancient DVD player that eats movie disks, etc. This works not only at the national and the international level, but also at the local level, depending on the audience you're writing for.

The Personal Problem - You may be the only person on the planet who has a problem with the fifth board on your picket fence, but it could be a potential source of humor. This can be tricky to write because, if people can't relate to your experience, they have to relate to you — or whoever the character is in your piece. You have to be a sympathetic character and play the fall guy for this to work.

Academic Drivel - Excessive jargon, legal, medical, computer, scientific or things like overblown titles and job descriptions are always good for a laugh. Handle these carefully, though, because you don't want to turn off large chunks of your audience. Remember, lawyers are people, too. Usually.

Statistics - A story containing statistics is good material. For one thing, despite what people say, statistics are always interesting. It's the shared experience thing again: It's neat to find out that, even though you *thought* you were the only one who liked eating sauerkraut on fudge, actually 53.2% of Americans do (Source: *The Compendium of Totally Fabricated Numbers Designed to Illustrate a Point*). Stats also provide material for small talk at parties, and it's the kind that makes you sound educated and well-read. There's also a faintly ridiculous element to statistics, as in who's the .2 person?

Trends - Sure, it's easy to look back now and snicker at bell bottoms and platform shoes. What about today's major movements? The nature of trends means that nearly everyone is doing the same thing, but nobody remembers until afterward to take an objective (skewed, warped) look at it. Sometimes people don't even realize it is a trend until somebody points out that everyone is doing it. Check out the magazines and TV shows that talk about what's hot and what's not.

Current Events - A major news item is another good source for humor. Be careful with being topical, though — unless you have a buyer that takes your material on a regular basis (like a weekly column, for example), you risk being out of date before you can sell it. Establish a presence in the markets with timeless (also known as evergreen) material first. Once buyers know your stuff, they'll take the current material while it's still fresh. In the meantime, keep the percentage of topical material in your portfolio relatively small or use current events for practice writing.

People - Listen to the way people talk, how they behave and what they complain about. Notice their quirks and foibles. If you plan to create funny characters for your book or report or whatever, the best place to look for inspiration is people. Base your creations on real idiosyncrasies, and you'll have believable characters. Diana Gabaldon's character Jamie (to whom I referred in Chapter One) has a habit of running his hand through his hair, which makes it stick up in all directions. It's just a little thing, but because you've seen someone, somewhere, do this, it makes him seem real. Do not write up your husband's/wife's habit of sneezing precisely three times in a row every time, though, without their permission — unless you are looking for a divorce. Putting your loved one's quirks out on display is an invasion of privacy and probably hazardous to your health. Make your characters composites, or give them habits, complaints or mannerisms that are based on something you've observed, but changed. Don't forget to notice trends or types of people, too.

Try to observe the common characteristics in, say, cab drivers, bartenders or teenagers. Tread *very* carefully with stereotypes – many are offensive, insulting, and for that matter just plain wrong. If you're going to venture into social commentary, it's probably best for you to poke fun at your *own* community. For example Anglo-Indian comedian Russell Peters has routine about his childhood with a traditional Indian father. He uses his father's accent, and gently pokes fun at his father's use of corporal punishment threats as a child rearing method. It's funny coming from him (although maybe not to his father!), but if someone with a different heritage tried the same routine about Anglo-Indians, it wouldn't be funny at all.

Animals - We all love animal stories — dogs that climb trees, cats that watch TV, turtles that play in your soap dish. Pet and animal stories are a perennial favorite and are likely to generate laughs and probably an "Aw, isn't that cute" as well. Observe the animals in your life as keenly as you would the people. Pick out the unusual aspects and report on them in a funny way. The fact that your dog digs holes in your yard isn't funny unless he does it with a shovel or buries your underwear. If something is a perennial favorite, that means that the topic is popular but also that it's been done before. Be original.

Relationships - Tons of material has been generated from observing all kinds of relationships. There's husband/wife, father/son, mother/daughter, friend/friend, boss/employee, not to mention all the relationships fostered through divorce, remarriage, adoption, the post office and the Internet. Wherever people interact, there's a story. The comic strip *For Better or For Worse* by Lynn Johnston is based strictly on one family and their immediate friends and co-workers. Despite a relatively limited cast of characters, the strip flourished for years and remains funny. Again, if you're going to write about you and yours, check with them first.

Sports - Picture it: You have several grown men being paid millions of dollars, standing on fake grass and sand, one group trying to throw the ball, the other trying to hit the ball, all while spitting and scratching themselves in unmentionable places. Tell me you see the comic possibilities here? 'Nuff said.

Advertisers - There's a TV ad running locally that talks about illiteracy. "If you have a reading disability or never learned how," it says, "we can help. Look us up in the Yellow Pages under Learn." As Dave Barry used to say, "I'm not making this up." Similarly, ads that seriously discuss "male itch" also invite (and perhaps deserve) jocularity. Beware of actually naming names because companies protect their trademarks with fleets of lawyers. Otherwise, go for it.

GREAT. I'VE GOT A FILE STUFFED FULL. NOW WHAT?

Now's the time to start looking for humor potential. Pick a few likely candidates — clippings or notes you really liked or felt strongly about. Grab a notepad and jot down whatever comes to mind.

OOH, GOOD ADVICE THAT. WHAT IF NOTHING COMES TO MIND????

Er, right, I was getting to it. That's the next chapter. In the meantime...

TIME OUT FOR GOOD BEHAVIOR

Enough reading, it's time for your homework assignment. This week, I want you to do the following things:

1. Research a few humor writers, past and present, local and international, male and female. I mean it: Get a wide range! In point form, jot down the basics of who they were, what they wrote about, and why you found them funny — or, if you didn't like them, write down why not.
2. Over the next week, go through your media outlets and start your humor file. In a few words, justify why each is or could be funny. As a reverse exercise, justify why they couldn't possibly be funny.
3. Keep a daily log of humorous incidents in your personal life. If it's a slow week, try to think of things in your past that would serve as well. Try to remember or notice funny gestures, mannerisms, events, that sort of thing.

CHAPTER THREE

GENERATING FUNNY MATERIAL

In the last chapter, we talked about where to find sources of inspiration and how to get yourself psyched up to write humor. Now we're going to get more specific. We're going to base this lesson and the assignment on the clippings and notes you've filed away, so if you haven't done your homework yet, please do so now and come back to this reading.

SO, WHAT'S THIS FRAME OF MIND THINGY?

When you read the work of other humor writers, did you notice what they all had in common? I hinted at it a few times when I was telling you where to look for ideas. No?

What all humor writers have in common is a different perspective. They have developed the ability to step outside themselves, the relationship, the trend, whatever, to take an objective look at their topic. People have told me I have a warped or skewed way of looking at things, and that's good because that's how funny material is generated.

How did I get this point of view? Well, one theory contends I was dropped on my head as a child. I prefer to think that I honed the skills by using one or both of these methods to change my thinking on an issue:

Foreign Friends Come to Visit - Imagine that you're hosting an exchange student from another country, and this is their first visit to your country. They've never experienced anything like whatever you're going to write about. How would you explain it to them? What points seem perfectly obvious to you but would seem amazingly different to someone who hadn't grown up the same way you had?

(BIG HINT: Just because you imagine yourself talking to a foreigner does not mean you have to WRITE IN A LOUD VOICE SO THEY CAN UNDERSTAND YOU!)

Martian Dropping By - Think of yourself as an anthropologist from another planet. You've landed here, and your assignment is to study these weird things called humans. Your home world is, of course, far superior to Earth. How could these Earthlings improve things?

These are just two mental tricks that I use, but you might come up with something better. Just use whatever helps you reframe the issue in a way that it hasn't been thought of before.

Okay, now slip yourself into outsider perspective, chose 3–5 pieces from your clipping pile, and try to generate some original material.

BRAINSTORMING

First, determine why you thought the idea was worthy in the first place. Did you have a point to make? Several points? Jot them down right off the bat.

Having your point firmly in mind is important because, if you don't have one, your one-liners will fall flat and your longer pieces will wander off into unfunnyland. If you're looking to add humor to your book or short story, write down why the gesture/mannerism/event you noted appealed, and what you think it reveals about somebody. Does that revelation fit what you have in mind for your characters? Does it fit your plot, or will you have to really work to add it to the action? Don't throw stuff in willy-nilly just because it's funny; make sure it's relevant to your story. An odd event incorporated into an otherwise coherent plot will stick out like a sore thumb.

Second, determine what is, or what could be funny about it. Let's say the article you've chosen is about a burglar who got stuck in the ductwork of a building he was trying to rob, part of your job is done already. If your article is about, say, a very serious civil rights protest, well, your work is cut out for you!

But, all is not lost. While civil rights itself is not a funny topic, protests might be. Did it cause a traffic jam? What was humorous about the traffic jam? Were the protest placards misspelled? Were there protesters protesting the protest? Say the protest was about animal rights. What's incongruous about the setting/players? Were the protesters wearing leather belts? Eating beef sandwiches? Kicking away a stray dog? Take the topic, turn it around, look at elements that are hidden in the background. Check your humor theory list — what's surprising in this situation? Where's the configuration?

Try some idea associations. Protests. Political pressure. Campaigns. Bunting. Elections. Baby kissing and glad handing. Candidates. Protecting the candidates. FBI. CIA. Tall men in suits and dark glasses. The movie *Men in Black*, aliens, space ships and ray guns...

Whoa! How'd we end up here? Doesn't matter. If you stray from your original topic, don't panic — this is just a brainstorming session. Sometimes you'll start writing about one thing, find that it's not working at all, but it has given you good ideas for another topic. Since generation is the name of the game, go with it. You can organize your thoughts later; for now, let them flow. Be one with the issue.

When the idea-association well runs dry, try some word association. Using "civil rights protest", you might get things like: civil, uncivil, swivel, snivel, rights, rites, left, right wing, left wing, wingnut, protest, Protestant, Catholic...

Kick the topic around for a while. If nothing comes to mind, or if the stuff you're coming up with doesn't appear to have potential, then tuck it away for another time. Take another topic and start again. Don't be too hard on yourself, though, especially if this is your first attempt at writing humor. If some of your scribblings seem even remotely humorous, work with them. Your first works aren't going to be knee-slappers. They may even stink a little, but that's okay. It takes time and practice, practice, practice to get it right. The point right now is to learn how to think and see things in a funny way — without the use of hard drugs.

In all likelihood, discovering funny elements in a topic you've chosen won't be that difficult. After all, you've already put it through one filter — your attention span, and it made it through that because you felt it was interesting.

If after a few tries you still haven't got anything workable, backtrack a little. Did you read a few funny pieces before you sat down to brainstorm? How long have you been including humor in your reading list? Does the topic/event/mannerism you are attempting to write about really interest you, or do you feel obligated to tackle it? Are you working in a quiet place without interruption? (Writing anything, including a grocery list, is nearly impossible with kids nearby or the phone ringing off the hook.) How do you feel today? Are you fighting a headache?

Try changing locations, taking a walk to clear your mind, grabbing something to nibble on, whatever. If you have a headache or are fighting the flu, forget it — take a break and try again another day. Don't give up too easily because writing is all about discipline, after all, but don't try to force it either because you'll just frustrate yourself completely. If you're really stuck, ask someone to help get you started. Find someone to brainstorm with you. Who knows? Maybe you'll find a writing partner!

OTHER GENERATION TECHNIQUES

Still stumped?

Try putting yourself in the middle of the issue or situation. For example, if you read an article about an animal rights protest, try to imagine what it would be like to participate in one. This is a variation of the "outsider" perspective — get inside the event. How would you react to it? Make yourself the fall guy. Perhaps you got up this morning, and while cleaning up from supper the night before, you discovered the tuna you ate wasn't marked "dolphin safe"? What do you tell your friends? Maybe you have a secret weakness for mass-produced breakfast cereals. Or you stapled your hand to the protest placard by accident.

If you have fictional characters in mind that are already well-developed, toss them into a situation and figure out how they'd react. Try to visualize how they would handle it.

Now take the opposite tack. Leave the original characters, but change the setting. That burglar we talked about before? What if he broke into a building that turned out to be a ductwork manufacturing firm? He could be wandering for hours. What if the protest took place in Antarctica? How do you shout protest slogans when your teeth are chattering?

Change the time of the event. What events in our history are parallel to what you're thinking about right now? Perhaps that burglar is the great-great-great-great-etc.-grandson of another burglar who broke into one of the pyramids and got stuck in Khufu's passage.

Cast your mind back through the other humorous material you've read, seen or heard. Is there an old classic you could revamp here? The Abbott and Costello "Who's on first, what's on second" routine perhaps? Don't use other people's material line-for-line, but try applying it to your topic and see what kind of new spin you can get.

Once you have some ideas, it's time to...

CHOOSE A FORM

No doubt, you've come into this course with an idea of what you want to write to begin with. Perhaps you've always wanted to be a humor columnist, or maybe you wanted to write gags for the Sunday funnies. If that's the case, you already have a clear idea of what form your writing will take.

On the other hand, perhaps you don't have any firm ideas of what form you want to try, or you're looking to add variety or originality to one you have in mind. A column or blog post, for example, can be just a straight essay-type piece, with a standard beginning, middle and end, or it can be written up as a conversation between two people. Look around at all the other writing formats you run across every day for possibilities:

A Book Review - Make up a fictitious book about your topic and write a review about the book. Don't forget those little blurbs on the book jacket are good sources, too.

Dialogue - Although I usually use an essay format for my columns, I use mini-dialogues between made-up characters quite frequently. They convey lots of information quickly and compactly and help break up paragraphs to add variety to the pace. (This is the same reason reporters quote people in their stories — it adds another voice and makes it more interesting.)

A News Report - Would your topic do well as a mock news report? Which kind: print, radio or TV?

A Letter to Mom/Dad/Brother/Sister/Girlfriend/Husband/Partner - What if you were to write up your piece as an old-fashioned letter to somebody? Keep in mind the properties of a letter: It can be written on fancy stationery, in bad/good handwriting, or on stained paper. It has to be delivered by post, so it could be outdated, bent, broken, spindled or mutilated and so on.

A Play Script - Become dramatic. What if you had to put your topic up on stage? What kind of props would you use? Lighting? Makeup? What sorts of lines would be said? What about the actors — what types of people are they?

A Company Memo - How well would your topic work in corporate speak and managerial-ese?

An Email - You know what emails are like! Bad spelling, worse typing, informal language and more smilies and emoji than you knew existed.

A Webpage - Surf the net. There are plenty of mock-up or satire webpages out there. Microsoft is a common target for parody and satire, but there are others.

A Short Story - A cast of characters, a quaint setting and a major conflict or tragedy ... what more could a humor writer need?

An Encyclopedia/Dictionary Entry - If you had to write a definition for your topic, how would it go? How would you write an explanation for posterity in *Encyclopedia Britannica*?

Government Type Forms - Insurance, health care, driver's license, taxes, birth and death certificates, affidavits, subpoenas, warrants, guarantees — heck, just look in your file cabinet!

Wanted Poster - Which do you want your topic to be: dead or alive?

CD/Album Sleeves - Old school for sure, but can you use that format?

How-To - Books, pamphlets, assembly instructions, the list is endless.

Biographies/Autobiographies - Memoirs make for great parody material.

Recipes - A cup of this, a dash of that, put it in the oven and bake until done.

Lyrics/Poetry - Can you sing for your supper? Rhyme for a reason?

Academic Journals - Those sometimes-obscure reports on the quality of clay pottery in 5th century Madagascar might be good for a chuckle or two. Might. Hey, it's a niche – check out Sh*t Academics Say.

Movie Trailers - Look, you know you see at least ten of them before they get around to the feature presentation. So why not use them? Short sentences, breathless descriptions, sharp dialogue, and sound effects to boot.

Software Manuals/Computer Languages - If you can figure your way through your Dell or Apple computer, perhaps you can use computer-related formats for your work.

WATCH YOUR TONE, YOUNG MAN/YOUNG LADY!

Once you've got an idea on the format you'd like to try out, then you need to decide on the tone you want to achieve.

What do I mean by tone? The best way to illustrate this is to check out the humorists from different time periods. Compare someone like Mark Twain or Voltaire with a writer of today. See any differences?

The creative work of any period tends to reflect the mood of the times. Voltaire, a French writer of the early 1700s, wrote criticisms on religion, government, and society. His *Candide* is a sardonic, occasionally sarcastic, but always witty look at the problem of evil in the world. His writing is pointed, whimsical, critical, and more or less optimistic. Overall his tone is gentle and hopeful. His style of writing is lyrical and eloquent, and he takes his time.

Fast forward to the 1990s, and the tone is a bit sharper, perhaps more cynical and jaded. In many cases, there is an element of pessimism, possibly because of the geopolitics of our time, which has a big psychological effect on society. The style of writing is punchy, fast-paced and, in some cases, raw. Dennis Leary, a stand-up comedian who has done commercials and starred in movies like *The Ref*, is a good example of this. What would you say the tone is right now?

Not every comedic writer takes this approach, of course. There were cynics in the 1700s, and there are optimists now. The point is that you should be aware of the overall trend in comedic writing and decide whether you want to go with that or against it. That decision has to do with whatever points you're trying to make, how you feel personally, and what the market will bear. If you go against the trend, you might have to fight to get your work accepted; on the other hand, it might be perceived as a breath of fresh air and the Next Big Thing. Go with the trend, and you might have an easier time of it, or you might be sloughed off as just another aspiring humorist.

Speaking of markets, don't forget to...

VISUALIZE YOUR AUDIENCE

Unless you plan to write strictly for your own amusement, then you have to keep your audience in mind at all times.

For example, there's no point in writing up a piece full of computer jokes and Internet wisecracks, if your audience is a group of elderly women who sigh wistfully over the war days when they were knittin' mittens for Britain. It's also probably not a good idea to submit Pope jokes to the local diocese newsletter.

Of course, there are elderly ladies out there who could web surf circles around you and me, and some of the best Catholic jokes I've heard have come from nuns. The point is: Know who you're writing for.

Throughout this course, I've referred to several writers, TV shows, movies and songs. You'll notice I've chosen a wide variety of them. You may be a big *Saturday Night Live* fan, but have never seen *Monty Python's Flying Circus*. I tried to accommodate that in my choice of examples. I have made one assumption, though — did you catch what it was? I've assumed that all of you are at least partially familiar with modern "Western" culture. Given the all-pervasiveness of that culture, the odds are good that at least one example will ring a bell, but there may be a few of you out there who missed every single reference I've made. It's something you have to think of when you're writing — especially when you're writing for a large, general audience. (If it helps, you'll probably be able to find clips of most of what I've talked about on YouTube.

If you research your audience, you might have a better idea of what they'd find funny, what they would find offensive, and what will simply go over their heads. Not only will this help you get more laughs more often, but it will save you time and money when the time comes to try to sell your work (more about that in Chapter Six).

DING! THERE'S THE RECESS BELL!

Your assignment for this week is to take those 3–5 pieces from your humor file, shift into outsider perspective and do some brainstorming. Once you've generated some ideas, go ahead and draft some rough work. If you're writing short material like jokes and one-liners, come up with about a dozen. If you're doing a longer piece like a blog post, just one will suffice, and they generally run 600–900 words. If you're working on characters or plot elements, come up with two or three. Good luck!

CHAPTER FOUR

MAKING IT SCHTICK

So, you're thinking, it's all very well to say, "generate some ideas and write something funny," but are there specific techniques out there to ratchet up the chuckles? You bet.

In this reading assignment, we're going to take a look at the methods of the masters. There are ways to set up comic situations, play with words and reverse expectations that are proven hits. There're lots of them, so let's dive right in, shall we?

TECHNIQUES

The Misunderstanding - How many sitcoms have you seen where the whole episode centers on a miscommunication of some kind? A package is delivered to the wrong house, someone has the timing of a meeting wrong, there is a mistaken identity, or someone has heard a false rumor about a person. The misunderstanding works because the *audience* knows the players are headed in the wrong direction, and they have fun anticipating the outcome. It involves incongruity (because the characters involved are working at cross-purposes) and surprise because the confusion can generate unusual results.

There are a few things to keep in mind when using the misunderstanding as a device. For starters, it is a common feature of sitcoms, so unless you can keep the confusion fresh and well-paced, the results might seem predictable. You must also bring about a resolution because leaving a misunderstanding unsolved will have your audience saying, "So what's the point?" Tie up your loose ends, and give your audience that all-important "closure." (How's that for psychobabble?)

I also recommend that the resolution be a good one for the characters involved. For example, if your misunderstanding was the result of one character's stupidity or a bad deed, a comeuppance is great, but don't overdo it. If the confusion ends up in a character's death, serious injury, or harsh emotional consequences, you risk leaving your audience with a sour taste in their mouths. Stephen Leacock tells us that "the very essence of humor is that it must be kindly." Your characters should achieve a redemption of sorts; otherwise, you can negate all the good feelings you've just worked so hard to generate. Unless you're looking for major shock value, remember that old saw: It's only funny until someone loses an eye.

Incidentally, misunderstanding isn't just a comedic device. You'll find it in tragic pieces as well. Indeed, nearly every major plot point of *Sons of Anarchy* centered on misunderstandings (based on lack of communication or outright lies).

Authority Punctured - Why are politicians, lawyers, clergymen, and educators so often the target of our barbs? We seem to feel better if we deflate egos now and then.

These are people who ordinarily have power over certain aspects of our lives. A politician, for example, sets policy and speaks on our behalf in the government. We go to a lawyer when we've gotten ourselves in trouble with the law. Clergymen are our contact points with the divine. We might feel inferior to these people, and making fun of them helps ease the tension created by that feeling of inferiority.

Skewering the powerful also serves another useful purpose: It makes us think critically about their position and influence. What's one of the first freedoms to go in a dictatorship? The right to make cracks about the dictator, of course! Deflating authority prevents us from being blinded to whatever real flaws there might be in the office or the person holding it.

Take a look at your clippings file and determine if there is a person or institution that warrants a few wisecracks.

Name Play - One specific way to puncture authority figures is to play with their names.

In Canada, there was a politician whose name was Preston Manning. He once represented a right-of-center conservative party; physically, he tends to look like a mild-mannered church minister. A commentator often referred to him as "Parson Manning," a play on his name that at once sums up his character and pokes fun. This same commentator (Alan Fotheringham) referred to the US as "The Excited States" and to government workers as "Swivel Servants" or sometimes "Snivel Servants."

This technique is extremely effective because it's short and punchy. It hits readers almost on the fly — they'll be reading along, following the main thrust of your sentence, and zing! There's a sudden, very illuminating comment. So, try figuring out the obvious characteristics of who or whatever you're trying to joke about, and see if there's some word play that works with their name or title. Don't forget to play with institutional acronyms, too.

Opposite - How many times have you heard the phrase: "When a dog bites a man that is not news. When a man bites a dog, that's news!"

The same goes for humor. What in your clippings file can be turned around? Are there any hypocritical elements, for example? How about the "financial adviser" who promises to help you make millions, but, whoops, is not in fact a millionaire himself? How about a vacation experience that turns out to be more arduous than the employment you were taking a break from? Take your topic and hold it up in front of a mirror. How does it look in reverse? (Answer: cipot ruoy.)

Irony - This is where you refer to someone or something as something they are most definitely not. Some examples include: Calling someone who is 6'6" and 275 lbs. "Tiny." Naming a road "Bentpath," when it is actually straight as a pin.

Slang in the Midst of Seriousness - When you have a particular style or rhythm going, sometimes stepping out of it briefly can be surprising and therefore funny.

Consider the following excerpt, which discusses a book about the Russian scientist Pavlov (he's the guy who discovered that if you ring a bell every time you feed a dog, the dog will learn to salivate whenever he hears the bell because he associates it with dinner):

"This wretched book is filled with terms like 'discriminated operants,' 'semantic conditioning,' 'generalization gradients,' 'variable ratio intervals,' and my personal favorite: 'differential reinforcement of successive approximations.' All of which neatly hides the fact Pavlov spent his entire career trying to get dogs to goober on command."

The word "goober," a slang term for "salivate," is jarring, particularly after all that scientific jargon. It's also a funny-sounding word. Oh yeah, there's another technique...

Funny-Sounding Words - No matter what our age, we are tickled by words and sounds that are foreign to our ears. For example, consider the following piece by Lewis Carroll:

'Twas brillig, and the slithy toves

Did gyre and gimble in the wabe:

All mimsy were the borogroves,

And the mome raths outgrabe.

"Beware the Jabberwock, my son!

The jaws that bite, the claws that catch!

Beware the Jubjub bird, and shun

The frumious Bandersnatch!"

Huh?

Do we have any idea what "vorpal" means? What it is to "gimble"? Nope. Yet, in spite of the fact a good chunk of this excerpt from *Through the Looking-Glass* is pure nonsense, we get the drift. Moreover, the poem is made more interesting because of the odd words.

Occasionally, I'll make reference to the planet Neefnoof in my work (hasn't everyone heard of this important astronomical discovery?) and a guy who comes from that well-known Russian republic of Urdismakovichshmedistan.

It doesn't have to be made up words, though — sometimes plain ol' non-English ones will do. Like slang in the middle of seriousness, a foray into another language can be funny. There is a somewhat obscure Silvester Stallone movie called *Oscar*, where Stallone is playing a gangster trying to go straight. His lead henchman ends up pulling butler duty for the day and has to answer the door several times. Normally, he speaks with a typical gangster accent, complete with the "deese, dem and dohs," but at one point, he opens the door, sees the visitor and says something like, "Youse is back again, huh? *Quel surpris.*" Of course, he mangles the French, but the line works because you don't expect an American gangster to speak French at all.

For another example, consider how many Yiddish words we've brought into the English language: schmuck, schmozle, putz, meshuggenuh. They sound odd to English ears and, provided your audience is likely to either know what they mean or guess from the context, they can be very effective.

Carry an Idea to the Extreme/Exaggeration - Sometimes just exaggerating a point can make it seem funny because you emphasize how ridiculous it is. A column by Dave Barry uses this technique:

"Anyway, my point is that Beanie Babies are viewed by many collectors as a serious financial investment (Ross Perot currently has 83 percent of his money invested in Beanie Babies, with $276 million in Bongo the Monkey alone.)."

Obviously, Ross Perot did not have $276 million in Bongo the Monkey (or if he did, perhaps it's just as well he didn't win the US presidency). But, by exaggerating the supposed investment value of these little stuffed toys, Barry was pointing out the ridiculous element of the Beanie Baby trend. And maybe Perot as well.

Pointing Out the Obvious/Illuminating Stuff We Take for Granted - This is another extremely effective technique. While writing about cargo spills in the ocean recently, I used the following line:

"For example, consider an incident on February 13, 1997 where a 'rogue wave' (so called, I guess, because waves have never been known to heave ships around) caught a freighter...."

Here, I'm being a bit sarcastic and pointing out that waves obviously make for turbulence in the water, and so to call one "rogue" is kind of silly.

For another example, consider also those real estate ads we've all read: "Comes complete with formal dining room (as opposed to your casual dining room) and some furnishings, including an occasional chair (does this mean it's a chair occasionally and a footrest any other time?)."

If there's something mentioned in your source that we all take for granted, how can you use that to be funny?

Superiority - Your readers or listeners will laugh more if they feel superior to you. If you have something to say, for instance, about Christmas shopping nightmares, describe them with you as the fall guy. Make sure it's your feet that get run over by the shopping cart, your black eye from the wrestling match in the toy department, and your credit card that gets rejected at the cashier. Describing it in general terms is impersonal, and while your readers might recognize what you're talking about, they'll relate better if it happens to someone they know (you, the narrator) and will also feel better because, well, their Christmas shopping problems aren't that bad. (Of course, this particular topic will fail miserably with those obnoxious types that have all their Christmas shopping done in July. Fortunately, this kind of person is rare.)

Inferiority - If there's a way to evoke sympathy in your work, you might try using that. To go back to the Christmas shopping experience, describe your worries about the consequences of not being able to find The Toy of the Year: "I could just picture it. My daughter in front of the tree on Christmas morning, her big, blue, puddled-up eyes shimmering in the glow of the Noel-Matic Christmas Winky Lights (just $9.95), saying 'Daddy, why didn't Santa bring me Sing and Snore Ernie? Was I bad?'"

What self-respecting parent wouldn't go, "Awwwwww...?" No, it's not slap-your-knee hilarious, but it does evoke sympathy, and it will bring a chuckle and a smile to any parent that has either been there, or feared the experience.

The Power of Three - For some reason, humans like trios. Three seems to be part of the Natural Order of Things. Use the number three in setting up the timing and rhythm of your joke.

For example, use two straight lines and then the punchline:

"We own a 118-year-old home. We purchased it a few years back with the idea of restoring it to something resembling its original state. So far, the motto for this little endeavor has been: 'It's not just a job; it's a career.'"

By using two straight lines, you build up expectations and create a sense of anticipation. With a punchline on the third, you satisfy the expectation and surprise with what you've chosen to joke about.

Or use three jokes in a row:

"So, don't be surprised if you see my dogs out caroling this Christmas. Don't wince when they sing 'Oh Come, All Ye Furfull' or 'Dog Rest Ye Merry Gentlemen.' In fact, just offer them some egg dog, er, nog."

The first joke "primes the pump," while the second joke carries the momentum, and the third finishes the set.

Those joke formats we talked about before also often use the three-part format. It's no coincidence that "priest, rabbi, minister" jokes use three clergymen, or that light-bulb jokes often have a three-part answer.

Using the Text to Your Advantage - If your work is going to be presented in written form, what formatting effects can you use to help your presentation?

Thanks to word processors, there are all kinds of tricks available: boldface, italics, underlining and different fonts.

I sometimes use italics to *emphasize* certain words — this encourages the reader to pay attention to that word and to read the text at a certain pace. It also sounds more conversational and relaxed.

You can also use paragraph breaks to your advantage. For example, setting out a single sentence as a paragraph by itself can help pacing, create dramatic pauses (because the reader's eye must take a few moments to move from the end of the last paragraph to the beginning of the next), and single out a joke or effect that might otherwise be lost in the rush. Example:

"...there was also an entire piece about a long [golf] drive champion, who hits the ball so hard that the skin on his fingers splits.

"Go ahead, shudder, I'll wait."

Don't go overboard with these things, though, as too much of a good thing is still too much. Also, you have to make sure that your buyers are both able and willing to follow your prescribed format. Ebooks are notoriously hard to format consistently across devices, and formatting is often lost in translation in emails, RSS feeds, different browsers, and so on. There is nothing more frustrating than seeing your lines edited or unformatted in a way that flattens the joke.

Using the Presentation to Your Advantage - If your work will be presented in a visual or auditory format, don't forget to use the available effects there, too.

For example, if you're writing a stand-up routine, you have a huge range of options. There are gestures, facial expressions, body positions, and prop possibilities. A radio routine doesn't have the visual aspect, but can make use of sound effects, funny dialects, and voices. Again, don't overuse these, as a little can go a long way.

The Sound and the Fury — Wherever possible, use the active voice, rather than the passive voice in your writing.

Wha?

By passive voice, I mean this:

The ball was hit by the boy.

Active voice would have us write the same sentence this way:

The boy hit the ball.

See the difference? One sort of describes it in a roundabout, I'll-get-there-in-a-minute kind of way. The other includes action, hence, active voice. It's punchier, shorter and keeps up the pace.

Don't stop with using the active voice, though. What "actions" or sights, sounds and smells can you include in your writing? Try this on:

Version 1: The ball was hit by the boy into the pitcher's crotch.

Version 2: The boy hit the ball into the pitcher's crotch.

Version 3: The boy hit the ball. *Crunch*. Right into the pitcher's crotch.

Which is more effective? (Okay, guys, uncross your legs. We're done now.)

Wherever you have described something, see if there is a shorter sound, action, visual image, or smell that can be used to do the same job.

Puns - You know I had to go there. I personally encourage the use of puns wherever possible because, while everybody claims to hate them, you'll notice everybody also laughs (or groans) whenever they're used. In other words, they get a reaction, and that's what you're looking for.

Why do I like puns so much? I think they show a good command of the language. You have to be semi-literate to understand them, and literate to create them. (A good test of whether you have fluent command of a second language is when you can pun with it).

Definitions - Try redefining a common term in a way that really demonstrates what it's like. Such as:

Shopping: The act of spending several hours circling the parking lot aimlessly searching for a spot, followed by spending several hours circling the mall aimlessly looking for a pair of shoes.

Also, try the reverse. Make up a word for a common action, or apply an existing word to a new definition, like this:

CREAMATION:

n. Mangling the "open here" spout on a milk container so badly that one has to use the "illegal" side.

THAT WAS TERRIBLE. CAN WE PLEASE MOVE ON?

Sure, if you're that keen to get on with it, let's do so. Your homework for the week:

1. Take a look at the work of another humor writer and analyze it critically. Does the writer use a technique that wasn't mentioned here? If so, what was it, and can you provide an original example?
2. Go back to the rough pieces you drafted in the last chapter. Can you rewrite some or all of it to incorporate some of the methods we've discussed here? If you can, give it another go.

CHAPTER FIVE

TEXTUAL HARASSMENT

TicketaticketaTAP! You hit the "enter" button with a flourish and finish your rewrite. You scroll up to the top of the screen and start reading the wonderfully funny material that has just emanated from your brain. Except that ... it's not very funny. What happened? It seemed hilarious when you had it all in point form! Now it's just ... flat. What to do??

Jumping out a window is an option, I suppose, but that might bring your humor career to a bit of a standstill. Your other option is to edit your work.

Those of you who have edited your work — or, worse, have had it edited by someone else — might think that the window option is looking better all the time. Why? Think of writing in terms of building a brick house. You build a house by constructing four walls, carefully laying down one brick at a time, holding it all together with mortar you've mixed and smoothed and layered. You add special touches like windows and fancy doors, a beautiful roof and decorative shutters ... and then you realize it looks all wrong and you have to take it apart, brick by brick.

Disheartening thought, isn't it?

When you labor over your writing, it's just as hard to contemplate cutting words and revamping sentences. However, it must be done. In fact, it should be done, even if you're fairly happy with your first drafts. You need to learn to cast a critical eye over your work, tighten it up, and polish it until it gleams.

What follows are some tips on how to edit your own work. Some of it can apply to any type of writing, while the rest is specific to humor writing.

DID YOU TELL YOUR AUDIENCE IT WAS GOING TO BE FUNNY?

Humans are peculiar creatures. Occasionally, we need to be reminded what part of our brains we're supposed to be accessing.

When you hear the phrase "once upon a time," what does that mean? That's right: It's the signal for "Fairy Tale Approaching." When we hear that set of words, we immediately make connections in our minds to things like dragons, princesses, hobgoblins, and giants with really big vegetable gardens. Before the storyteller even gets to the second sentence, we're already in Official Fairy Tale Mode and we have an idea of how to react.

The same goes for humor. When you hear the phrase "Did you hear the one about..." what does that signify? Yep, a joke. You already know a punchline is en route before it arrives.

That's not to say you should preface everything you write with "Did you hear the one about..." because, man, that gets old. But always keep the conventions of your particular writing format in mind. If you're writing a humor column, did you title it with something funny? If you're writing those lightbulb jokes, did you use the standard opener for that type of wisecrack? If you're writing a story and you want people to know one character is supposed to be funny, do your other characters react to him/her appropriately? Do they foreshadow his/her jocularity? If your other characters don't laugh at him/her, how can you expect your audience to?

If your intent is to surprise people with a joke, then giving the Funny Alert is not a good plan. You'll have to judge whether your comedy is strong enough to catch your audience's attention, or whether they'll end up saying, "Oh, was that a joke?"

TIMING AND STRUCTURE

Timing, as you've probably heard somewhere along the line, is a key element of comedy. Just like with sword play, you have to know when to thrust, dodge, turn, and parry.

The timing of your work is likely a product of the structure you laid down in the first place.

Let's look at a few short formats first.

If you're writing a series of one-liners, where have you placed the kicker or punchline? This format almost always places it at the end. One-liners are so short that you have to use the first bit of your sentence for setup. The following examples work because of brevity and good structure:

What do you get if you do not pay your exorcist promptly? Repossessed.

French gourmet BBQ: haute dog.

If you are a sheep rancher on the move, do you carry your livestock in a ewe-haul truck?

These examples aren't as effective because they have the wrong structure:

Why don't we have cultured oil anywhere ... instead of only crude oil?

Test: To see if your mission on earth is complete. If you are still alive, it isn't.

Was your uncle who died a band or an orchestra conductor? No: lightning.

These lines could be funnier if they were rearranged.

What about longer formats? Well, let's talk about funny anecdotes. Where have you placed the funny part of the story? Usually, we hold the amusing part until either the very end or close to it because we need to set up the gag or joke; it also helps build suspense and expectations. A funny story that works might look like this:

A miserable man, obviously feeling ill, went to the doctor. The doctor examined him thoroughly and then gave him the reassuring diagnosis.

"Well, there's absolutely nothing wrong with you except that you're overstressed," the doctor said. "What you need to do is forget your work, enjoy yourself, go out and have a good laugh. Why don't you go out and see that new comedian they're all talking about?"

"That's great doc," said the man, "except I'm that new comedian they're all talking about!"

Fairly simple story, not too hard to mess up, right?

Wrong.

What if you started it like this?

"There's this comedian that's all stressed out and feeling pretty awful. Anyway, he went in one day to a doctor's office and...."

By letting the cat out of the bag so early, we've ruined the joke. Unless you can find a way to sustain the humor all the way through, you've got to reorganize.

On the other hand, don't spend too long in the setup either. Consider this:

"There's this guy who was feeling really sick. Not deathly ill or anything, but I mean, to look at him, you could tell he was pretty low. He wasn't sure what he had, and he figured it wasn't serious, but he had to do something. (Yawn.)

"So, he went to this doctor, who looked him up and down, took his blood pressure, applied the stethoscope, checked his temperature, weighed him and did the whole examination thing. (YAWN)

"After all of this examination, the doctor said, 'Well, your blood pressure checks out okay, your weight is well within specified parameters, your heart sounds pretty good. You're not on any drugs, and you said that you hadn't been experiencing any headaches. (ZZZZZZzzzzzz!)"

At this point, your punchline must blow the audience out of their seats, or else they'll be asking themselves, "Was this trip really necessary?"

How about longer pieces, like humor columns or blog posts?

I like to think of a humor column as a funny essay, and I try follow an essay type structure: intro, body, and conclusion. Or, in the words of a chemistry teacher I once had (and this wasn't original to him):

"Tell 'em what you're going to tell 'em,

"then tell 'em,

"then tell 'em what you told 'em."

You don't *have* to follow this format, but be aware that if you don't have some sort of structure in mind, you risk wandering off course.

Where are the jokes in your column? Are they all in the first three paragraphs? If so, your audience may end up being bored by your work by the time they finish, and they might not come back. Are they all in the last three paragraphs? There's a chance they might not have the patience to wade through the slower bits to get to the good stuff. Wherever you can, spread out the laughter. Keep an even pace, punctured by the occasional extra-strong zinger.

The same goes for funny characters in a story. Where did you reveal all her foibles? Expose her entire character early on in the book, and she becomes uninteresting. Half the fun of reading a longer work is discovering new things about the people involved along the way. Spread out the revelations! Oh, and don't forget consistency. If your character has a habit of, say, laughing at inappropriate moments at the beginning of the book, but you fail to carry this on (and don't account for the loss of habit by character growth), you're being inconsistent. Worse, if you have her doing something nasty toward the end of the book, you negate your humorous character-building efforts!

CUT THE NUMBER OF WORDS

Ask yourself: Why does a diamond sparkle?

Precious stones sparkle because they're cut in a certain way and polished. Raw diamonds are generally boring-looking glassy lumps. Jewelers cut away large portions of the raw diamond and give it sharp corners, small, multiple facets, and polish the result.

Why does good writing sparkle? The answer is the same: snip, snip, snip. Hack it to pieces. Be brutal. Be ruthless. It's chainsaw time!!!

GULP! OKAY, BUT WHERE DO I START?

Look for the deadwood. If the sentence or paragraph isn't either a setup or a punchline, it's probably expendable. Here's a deadwood checklist:

The Joke/Anecdote/Column/Character Revelation Has Moved Backward Instead of Forward - How often have you heard someone tell you a story that starts out at one place, but jumps around before it gets back to the original point? As in, "This guy went to the doctor, right? The day before ... or maybe it was the day before that ... anyway, the day before he'd made the appointment because he'd felt really tired. Last week, you see, he'd noticed dark circles under his eyes...." Whoa! First of all, is any of that detail really necessary? If it is, then for goodness sake, start at the beginning and go from there. If not, axe it!

The Joke/Anecdote/Column/Character Revelation Has Too Many Narrators - "My first cousin's husband's stepsister said to me...." Argh! Unless your point is about families, the audience does not need — or care — about your family tree. Cut the number of narrator and voices.

Constantly Telling People How Funny They'll Find the Joke/Anecdote/Column/Character Revelation - "So there's this guy, right? You'll love this ... he's going down the road ... really, you won't believe this ... and he meets this chicken ... laugh ... and this chicken says ... oh God, this is funny...." In this case, you've given your audience two choices: A) Slap you and say GET ON WITH IT! or B) Leave.

OTHER WAYS TO SLASH AND BURN

This checklist applies to all writing, not just humor writing:

Redundancies - Have you said the same thing twice or two times in a row? Kind of like I just did? Get rid of these things. They are life-sucking parasites in any work. Examples:

Mutual cooperation - can't have cooperation unless it's mutual, can we?

Violent explosion — er, is there any such thing as a mild explosion?

Past history - unless you're watching a certain Michael J. Fox movie, there isn't any future history!

Weather conditions - it's either weather, or it's conditions, but not both.

Tautology - The repetition of the same words, or use of synonymous words in close succession. The wordy examples and their svelte cousins:

and so as a result - and so

each and every - each

pair of twins - twins

when and if - when

Circumlocutions - A fancy way of saying "talking around it." Be direct!

ahead of schedule - early

am in possession of - have

at an early date - soon

call a halt - stop

Trite Expressions or Clichés - Clichés are phrases we've kept around because they work. They have their place in writing because they can sum up situations in a compact and recognized way. However, they can be overused, especially in news reports. How many times have you heard about police making a "grisly discovery"? Fighting takes place with a "hail of bullets," and jets always "scream overhead." Cut these.

OTHER CLEVER WAYS TO STEP ON YOUR OWN JOKES AND FLATTEN YOUR COPY

Excessive Satire - When you emphasize the bad points about a situation, you can make a point and generate some laughs. When you overemphasize the bad points, you can drain the humor out of a situation. Satire degenerates into sarcasm. Unless you plan to make mean-spiritedness your trademark, lighten up. Avoid preaching to your audience.

Going for the Lowest Common Denominator - Yes, burping does generate laughs. There will always be a portion of the public that enjoys that kind of thing; some will even laugh at the same burp several times in a row.

The problem is, that kind of humor isn't particularly original, nor does it take much effort. On the whole, the humorists that leave an enduring mark — the ones we think of as classic comedians — usually go beyond that style. Furthermore, they don't mix radically different styles very much. When you throw low-brow yuks into a middle or high-brow piece, you're doing a disservice to all three audiences. Middle and high will be offended by low, while low will find the middle dull and the high pretentious. Remember your target audience and mix accordingly.

Belaboring a Point - Up to three jokes on the same subject can be funny. Anything more than that can become repetitious and annoying. For example, consider a series of jokes that start out with "The air in New York is so dirty that..." and moves on to "Yes, in fact, it's dirty enough to..." and keeps going with "The air is so darn dirty that it...." After a while, your audience is going to say, "WE GET IT!!!" This is especially important to remember if you're doing more personal or critical jokes like "My mother is so darned fat that..." because this goes from funny to downright cruel very quickly. Speaking of cruelty...

Non-Constructive Humor - Humor, as I've mentioned before, can be a type of criticism. If used well, it can be very helpful and possibly constructive. If used badly — e.g., a joke that is racist or sexist — it just hurts the targets and makes other people angry. In my view, humor should always be positive in intent. Otherwise, you will offend without doing anybody any good. Remember the medical motto: Do no harm.

Another example is referring to a politician with a rude or insulting nickname. It's a useful (although probably dangerous) way to puncture authority in genuinely despotic regimes, where there isn't a free press. *Routinely* using rude nicknames for all politicians in a democracy diminishes the technique's effectiveness and isn't constructive. Context is important!

Using Words You're Not Familiar With or Comfortable With - If you're not sure about the meaning of a word, look it up. If you can't be bothered looking it up, get rid of it. Misusing it will just make you look silly. Or worse, you'll use a term that's offensive and hurtful to members of your audience.

If you or someone you're working for will be reading this material aloud (e.g., a speech or stand-up routine), make sure the words are easy to say. You have no idea what stumbling over unfamiliar words can do to timing and delivery!

CLEVER WAYS TO IMPROVE YOUR WRITING

Be Yourself - Don't attempt to take on someone else's style. Study it, learn from it, *maybe* even incorporate a few elements of it into your own work. Just don't try to force yourself to write just like another humorist. Style is as varied and individual as people themselves. You've got a style; you've just got to develop it.

Short Sentences/Short Paragraphs - Diamonds have small, multiple facets, and humor should have small, multiple facets. Break up run-on sentence into two or three shorter bits. Liven up the pace with shorter paragraphs.

Adopt a Conversational Tone - As you may have noticed with this course, I've tried to be very conversational. My tone and style would be much more formal if I was teaching something like psychology or mathematics. Humor is a more casual writing form (notice I said "casual," not "careless" — it is a studied nonchalance, after all) and should be somewhat informal. Being conversational implies relaxation, the sharing of common ground, perhaps even a certain intimacy. To make your audience laugh, you must connect.

PASSING THE BUCK

Once you've reviewed your work and ripped it to bits, take a deep breath and hand it to someone to read. It's time to get a second opinion.

Some tips about handing out your work:

Make sure you give your work to someone you trust, especially if this is your first attempt at the genre. Determine if they will give you an honest, *objective* opinion that is constructive. If you suspect they'll skim it and say, "This is great, dear," to spare your feelings, don't bother. Likewise, if they're likely to get "editor's glint" in their eye and break out the knives, run the other way! You need a fair assessment, not ego-building or ego-shredding.

1. Do not hover while they review it. Leave the room, go for a walk, take up knitting. There is a huge temptation to watch their reactions, I know, but *don't* do this to yourself or to them. They'll either fake reactions to please you, or be so nervous about laughing at the wrong bits they'll get angry with you.
2. Do not argue with their assessment! Even if you totally disagree with it, keep it to yourself. It's safe to ask them why they didn't think a bit was funny because you can learn from that. However, if they

have to defend their opinions, they'll never give you one again.

3. Don't take it personally. This is a tough one. You've shed blood, sweat and tears over this stuff. It's hard to take criticism when there's so much emotional investment, but it has to be done. If you write for a living, you know you need a thick skin. If you plan to write for a living, then you'd better develop one, fast. Especially if you plan to work in comedy!

4. If you can't follow the advice above, then don't hand the material out to friends and family. It's bad enough that you've locked yourself away from them for hours at a time to struggle over a keyboard or a notepad. Do not add insult to injury by getting hurt, argumentative or just plain annoying over critiques! It's not worth breaking up good relationships, so take it to a tutor or join a writing group. It's less personal there.

5. If you *can* follow the above advice, then take your work to more than one person. Remember, I told you that everyone has a different sense of humor. While your spouse may not think a particular line is funny, your brother might bust a gut laughing over it. Different strokes for different folks.

6. This is a big one: Learn that you will never be able to make *everyone* laugh, and you will never be able to please everyone either. While there may be some people who fall over laughing even for your throwaway lines, there will be other

people who either just don't get your brand of humor or actively dislike it. And that's okay! You just need to learn to write for *your* audience and not worry about the rest.

WOW, THIS IS TOUGHER THAN I THOUGHT. CAN WE CALL IT A DAY?

Don't forget the homework!

1. Apply what you've learned from this reading to your own work and, yes, rewrite it again. Edit it unmercifully.
2. Once you've done that, if you can handle the heat, pass the work out. Take note of the bricks and bouquets you receive. What did you learn from the experience? Rework your piece again if necessary.

CHAPTER SIX

IT'S TIME FOR THE PITCH

You made it through the editing process! Now you have one or more honed, polished and positively gleaming bits of humor. You can make Aunt Griselda laugh just by waving these masterpieces under her nose. So, now what?

Now comes the hard part. Selling.

"Dammit, Jim, I'm a writer, not a salesman!" you say. Or, for those of you who don't watch *Star Trek*: "But, I am an artiste! A performer! Not a salesperson!"

Sorry, folks, but being a writer also means being in sales, and being in business generally. Until that fine day when you acquire a superb agent, you have to do all the hustling yourself — and even after you get an agent, it's always a wise idea to keep an eye on the scene just to make sure your representative is doing a good job. So, resign yourself, right now, to spending a good chunk of your time in marketing.

You should also resign yourself to the fact that there is no easy way to the top — or the middle or even the bottom, for that matter. Even if you are brilliantly funny, incredibly photogenic and get along well with kids and dogs, it's going to be a long, hard haul. The reality is that there are hundreds of other writers out there competing for attention, and there are a relatively small number of outlets for your work. There is no sure-fire way to get noticed, and despite what the media says, there is no such thing as an overnight success. Like the old phrase says, it's "One percent inspiration, ninety-nine percent perspiration."

Now let's look at some ways to make the struggle a little bit easier.

BELIEVE IN YOURSELF AND YOUR WORK

One of the first things you need to do before you start sending your work out is ask yourself, "Am I ready?"

If, for example, you hesitate to show your work to family and friends, and you cringe at the tiniest bit of criticism ... chances are, you're not ready. Go back to your desk, read some more, write some more and practice, practice, practice. There will always be a hint of trepidation when you hand over your creative work for review, but you need to develop confidence in your abilities.

Why are belief and confidence so important? Well, you slave over a piece, pour your heart and soul into it and work it into a thing of beauty and perfection. You search the market listings, pick out the ideal target, prep your manuscript, and send it away, full of visions of bylines, paychecks, cocktail parties and book-signings. And you wait. And wait. And wait. Did I mention wait? The industry is still very, very slow. Turnaround time on submissions can be two weeks, two months or, yes, even two years.

But lo! What's that in the inbox? Open it and find ... the dreaded rejection slip. Why? The magazine/publisher/newspaper and your work were perfectly matched, or so you thought. What does the rejection slip say? Usually, it's just a form letter. No thanks, not at this time. Sorry, doesn't meet our needs. Wanna know something? Most writers are thrilled to receive criticism of their work, even in a rejection — because at least it's a real live opinion and not an anonymous "not interested."

GADS, THAT'S DEPRESSING. WILL YOU LIGHTEN UP?

Sorry. I'm just trying to prepare you for the way things work. You need to develop an unshakeable faith and love for what you are doing in order to succeed. It takes courage to hear "no" all the time and still keep sending material out. You will make it — *if* you persevere. Develop a stubborn streak.

Do chin-ups to build up your stamina. Insult yourself once a day to build up a thick skin. Rid yourself of idyllic notions of lazy mornings at a writing cabin or furious bouts of creativity in a studio in upper Manhattan. Do not give up your day job.

When you are prepared to receive enough rejection slips to wallpaper your house, then you are ready to send out your material.

And keep sending it. Keep writing; keep working on new material. Send it, too. Talk to other writers. Read inspirational bits of information, like the fact that *Zen and the Art of Motorcycle Maintenance* was rejected something like 122 times before it was published ... and it hasn't been out of print since.

Don't ever give up because you will win. You will get there. And when you do, have a cocktail for me.

KNOW YOUR WORK

Okay, so now you're all psyched up and ready to face the beast. Do you know what you're sending out?

Take a good look at your work and try to classify it. Is it a series of one-liners? If so, where would that likely be appreciated? There's no point sending one-liners to a market that is looking for humorous essays. Would your one-liners work as T-shirt slogans? Bumper stickers, greeting cards? Or are they better for comic strips or stand-up comedians?

Is your work the first edition of a humor column? If so, can you write more? Could you be funny on a weekly basis? Who looks at humor columns?

Is it a funny book? What's the genre? Generally speaking, textbook presses don't have much use for humorous science fiction.

In other words, save yourself — and the publishers/editors you're submitting to — some time by having a clear understanding of *what* you're trying to sell. Speaking as someone who has done time as an editor, there are few things more frustrating in a busy day than to get material that is totally inappropriate to your publication. If you've got salespeople bending one ear and editorial types yelling in the other, you sure as heck aren't going to give the time of day to a writer who hasn't done their homework. Which brings us to:

FINDING MARKET INFORMATION

Once you know what it is you're trying to flog, you've got to determine where to send it. Now is the time to head to the library, the bookstore, talk to your writers' groups, and go online.

Let's start with books. If you want to save yourself some money and you have a decent library close by, look up a few "market" books. By this, I mean things like *Writer's Market*. Check under all the words related to your type of work: humor, markets, stand-up, cartooning, whatever. If this is the first time you've encountered these kinds of books, borrow them and take them home to study them thoroughly. Once you know what kind of information these books offer, then you can start photocopying, photographing, or writing down the important bits. Make sure it's a *recent* edition. Anything older than a year is suspect, and you'd be wasting your time with anything over two years old. Editors change jobs frequently. Companies also merge and relocate, so you'll be sending envelopes or emails off only to have them come back with "return to sender."

If you think you'll be sending out a lot of material on a regular basis, buying these books will be a good investment — you'll have them right at your fingertips. Or better yet, check out the online version. These usually involve a monthly fee, which can add up, but you might save yourself some time with faster search functions, and theoretically, these databases are up-to-date.

If the library or local bookstore doesn't seem to have much variety, check with any one of the hundreds of writing groups out there. Often, these groups put out their own market reports and have lending libraries full of writing reference books. There are also book clubs that offer specific membership deals and will send you catalogs periodically with the latest and greatest information. *Writer's Digest* has a club like this — membership information can usually be found in advertisements in their magazine.

Of course, we can't forget the Internet, which I personally think is the best thing to happen to writing since the invention of the ball point pen. There are literally hundreds of sites out there that have market information available 24 hours a day, 7 days a week — and ding! they're quite often free. Obviously, you have to be careful using information that is given out for free because there's less pressure to keep things accurate, but generally speaking these sites are operated by other writers who have the same concerns as you do. One that seemed reasonably up-to-date and well-regarded at the time of this writing was The Submission Grinder at https://thegrinder.diabolicalplots.com/Search/ByFilter.

The other problem to keep in mind with the Internet is that it's like eating potato chips: Once you start surfing, it's hard to stop. You click on one site and find that the webmaster has considerately searched and linked up half a dozen more sites, so you click on them and so on and so on ... and suddenly your tea has gone cold and half the morning is gone. My advice? Pick a site as a launch pad, investigate it thoroughly and then check out each of its links one by one. Bookmark those sites that look like they're updated frequently and might prove useful. There are lots of pretty sites with neato features, but unless they have information you're going to need, scrap 'em. Keep coming back to your original launch pad until you've exhausted the links there. Otherwise, you spend hours wandering, and you'll lose track of other sites that you thought might be good bets.

PAY ATTENTION TO WHAT THE MARKET INFORMATION TELLS YOU

Once you have your market reference materials, read the information they give you and pay attention to details. Let's look at a typical market listing for reference:

GOLF BOY—The Publisher's PO BOX 1234, Salt Lake City UT 84151-0366. Email annee@thegolfboy.com. Contact: Anne Editor. 50% freelance written. Quarterly magazine. "Drive the fairway with Nicklaus, putt the green with Tiger, visit Pebble Beach. This magazine brings you all of this and more — tips from the pros, new equipment, rule and tour updates." Established 1996. Circ. 15,000. Pays on publication. Publishes mss an average of 6 months after acceptance. Byline given. Buys first North American serial and second serial (reprint) rights. Editorial lead time 2 months. Submit seasonal material 4 months in advance. Accepts simultaneous submissions. Reports in 1 month on queries; 2 months on mss.

Nonfiction: Historical/nostalgic, interview/profile, personal experience, technical, golf. Buys 8-10 mss/year/ Query with published clips. Length: 1000-1300 words. Pays $125-800.

Reprints: Accepts previously published submissions. Pays 50% of amount paid for an original article.

Photos: Send photos with submission. Reviews 4x5 transparencies (preferred), any size prints. Negotiates payment individually. Captions, model releases, identification of subjects required. Buys one-time or all rights.

Columns/Departments: Golf tips (for the weekend golfer). Personal experiences/nostalgia (for the average golfer), both 500 words. Buys 8-10 mss/year. Query with published clips. Pays $50-125.

So, what does all this tell you? Well, first it's obviously a golf magazine, so unless your piece has to do with golf, chances are they won't be interested. It gives you both an email address and a snail mail address, so you might be able to query by email (which is cheaper and generally faster). Since it's listed as being 50% freelance, you might have a chance selling to it. Some magazines rely strictly on staffers to fill their editorial needs. It is only a quarterly, however, so they're not likely to need tons of material.

What else does this listing tell us? It's a relatively old magazine, established in 1996. It has a decent circulation, although not huge. Here's an important bit: "pays on publication," followed by "publishes mss (manuscripts) an average of 6 months after acceptance." If you read further, you'll see that it reports in a month on a query (a letter that says "would you be interested in...") and two months on a complete manuscript (where you send in the piece without asking first). In other words, do not count on this sale alone to pay the rent. Assuming they accept, it will be about two months from submission date until you find out and another six months before your piece is published — yep, eight months later. They do give a byline, however, which means you'll see your name in print. As any published writer will tell you, that's half the fun, and you can start to build out your portfolio.

This listing also gives you a rough sketch of what the magazine is looking for. You'll notice it does not mention fiction or poetry, for example, so you're wasting your time sending that type of material to this magazine. There doesn't seem to be a lot of room for humor either, although you might get away with a funny "personal experience" piece on golf. Most listings recommend you check out issues of the publication to get a feel for the type of material they publish, and you *should* try to do that... through your library or free sample issues, or free articles online and/or browsing their website. Obviously, they want prospective writers to buy a copy of their publication, because they want to sell copies, but let's face it: you simply can't afford to buy everything you intend to query.

Annnyway, see where doing your homework can save you a lot of time and money? If you had just looked at the name and address of this magazine (and had not known what the *Golf Boy* reference meant), and fired off your piece, you could have wasted the time it took to prepare the manuscript and package it as well as the money it took to post it. Selling your work is expensive and time-consuming to begin with — don't add to your troubles.

BUT LOOK, HERE'S A GOOD ONE!

Okay so *Golf Boy* is out, but what if you've found a magazine called *One-Liners R Us*?

Well, if you've got some one-liners, then this might be a good starting point. Again, though, pay attention to what the market listings tell you. If it says it works only with established writers, you can try sending your material in, but your chances are slim unless you've been published elsewhere. If it says query first, then query first. If it says it accepts submissions only on 3x5 index cards, then send in your stuff on 3x5 index cards, even if you think it is stupid to have to do so in an era of digital communications.

If it specifies that it buys only new material (not reprints) and you've been lucky enough to have your stuff printed elsewhere, save your money and send your material to a place that does accept reprints. If the magazine title sounds promising, but the listing doesn't say much about submission protocols, it might be worth asking the publication for writers' guidelines.

Guidelines are a set of instructions that the publication has developed over the years to make the submission process more efficient. Pay attention to them and follow the directions. Editors and publishers who have to wade through heaps of mail probably won't even *look* at submissions that don't fit their guidelines. It's part of how they filter.

TO QUERY, OR NOT TO QUERY

If you have found a few good markets, then you can use a query to find out if they'd be interested in your work.

A query is a letter or email that briefly sets out who you are and what you're selling. There are entire books on writing "catchy" queries, and writers' markets also have tips on writing them, so I won't go into too many details here. Generally, though, the letter should be typed on clean stationery or in an email, be in a clear, easy-to-read font, and be professional in tone. Do not write a query with something like "Look, I got this funny stuff. Wanna see it?" Some tips for writing queries include:

- Limit yourself to one page, single-spaced.
- Address the editor by name whenever possible. Make sure you have the right person, and the right spelling of their name. If there's no name, be sure to get the right title.
- Try to catch the editor's interest with a strong opener.
- Indicate what kind of material you have, how long it is, and provide other relevant details (put yourself in an editor's shoes: What would you want to know about this stuff? What would make you buy it?).
- Let the editor know if you have any artwork or photography to accompany your piece and what format it's in.

- Mention any experience you have. If you don't have any, don't mention your lack of credits.
- Use a polite closing.
- Remember that they have to go through hundreds of queries, and that they're under tremendous deadline pressure. Try to place yourself in their shoes. How would you like to be treated or approached?

BASIC MANUSCRIPT FORMAT

If the option to query isn't listed, or you simply prefer to take your chances and send in a complete manuscript or perhaps even HURRAY! the queried editor has replied positively, then it's time to send in your work. Refer to your guidelines, market listing, or editor's reply for specific instructions on formatting your manuscript.

If there aren't any specific instructions, then you should follow the standard manuscript format, which is based on common sense. Editors and publishers want something that's easy to read, so type it out, don't use crazy fonts, and make sure you've proofread it. A good reference can be found at William Shunn's page here: https://www.shunn.net/format/story.html, but just searching online for the term "standard manuscript format" will give you what you need as well.

SEND IT!

Once you've prepped and polished, head to the post office or your email app and send it away.

It's a good idea to keep track of what you're sending to who and when. There are computer programs available to "track submissions," and if you're sending out lots of material, they might be worth investigating. Otherwise, a standard spreadsheet or old-fashioned notebook will do. Things to mark down include:

- whether it was a query or complete manuscript and the title of your work,
- the name of the publication you sent it to,
- the specific person you addressed in your mailout and the date you sent it out, and
- the approximate time you can start looking for a response.

AND NOW ... FEGGEDABOUDIT!

Do yourself a favor and do not spend the next several weeks haunting the post office or refreshing your email inbox. Forget about whatever you just mailed out and get back to work. Keep practicing, keep reading, and above all, keep writing and sending stuff out.

Every once in a while, you can check your submissions and see if you should be doing any follow-ups. Bear in mind that the report times given in market listings are usually approximate guidelines. Time varies according to the season (Christmas holidays? Forget it until the New Year), workload of the editors involved, the size of the magazine (the bigger the market, the more manuscripts they receive) and so on.

Allow some leeway, and don't panic if you haven't heard back from the market in the precise amount of time the listing noted. And only follow-up when a listing expressly says it is okay to do so. Remember, editors get hundreds of queries. You'll be lucky to get an autoresponder or form letter response.

It helps to compare the process of getting (traditionally) published to the process of making wine. It takes quite a while for a grape vine to mature enough to start producing grapes. It takes another long while to get the fruit harvested, pressed, blended, and into barrels for aging. In other words, the work you're doing now likely won't produce results – a fan base, cash in hand – for a few years.

DEALING WITH REJECTION

It happens. Often. How do you deal with it?

As I noted before, talk with other writers. Join a local group, chat online, sign up to an email list. Writing can be a lonely experience, but it is made easier by sharing concerns and tips and tricks with like-minded people. You'll feel better, you might learn something — heck, you may even get a lead on a new market.

Read and do things that inspire you. If walking in a meadow lifts your spirits, do that often. If reading poetry does it for you, haul out the anthology.

Be persistent. When a manuscript comes back to you, don't stuff it in a desk drawer. Immediately — the same day, if possible — choose another market and send it out again. Writing is kind of like riding a horse: If you get thrown off, you have to get right back on, or else you'll become too scared to go on. Remember that there is always a chance your work will be used/published if you have it on the market. There is *no* chance if it languishes on your desk.

REVIEWING YOUR MATERIAL

The temptation is strong when you get a rejection to look at your material and say, "What's wrong with it?" or even "What's wrong with me?"

While remaining objective is important, don't get into the habit of second-guessing yourself. It makes rejections that much more depressing, and it also invites self-doubt. These are not good feelings.

Resist the temptation to reread your material *every* time it comes back to you. If you've just started sending out the piece, then keep sending it out — don't agonize over it. Only review your work about once every 3—4 months. This will allow you to get some distance from the piece and give you "fresh" and objective eyes. Hopefully, in the meantime, you will have written more material, have practiced, and gained experience. When you review with both distance and experience, you will be able to say one of two things about your work:

1. No, I still think this is good material. It deserves a home.
2. Hmm, this is rough. I can do this, this and this to fix it. Then I can send it out again.

The first thought indicates confidence tempered with the wisdom of repeated practice. The second thought indicates growth and development. Both are great things to have.

CAN'T I JUST PUBLISH IT MYSELF?

You absolutely can!

You can write a blog, start a humorous Facebook page or Twitter account, produce Tik Tok videos (or whatever platform is hot when you're reading this) or package your material up into a book. You can get directly in front of potential readers or viewers, today. Many people are getting their start this way.

Some stay indie published and make a good living at it. Others get picked up by traditional venues. Still others do both. Putting your work "out there" also gives you a chance to get real feedback from people who can be objective, which helps you hone your work faster.

That's the good news. And make no mistake, it *is* good news. It's empowering and provides unprecedented opportunities.

The bad news is that you'll have to spend a fair amount of your time learning your chosen platform: how to use it, how to use it *well*, testing your material, and figuring out how to get readers or followers. You'll also need to learn about branding, positioning, marketing, and advertising.

As you might suspect, this will entail an outlay of cash as well as time. You're effectively becoming a 'solopreneur,' at least at the beginning.

Now, some people thrive on this sort of thing. They like being in control of their own destinies, and they love learning and hustling. Other people feel utterly overwhelmed by the idea of having to do *everything* themselves, and would much rather just produce content. There's probably a third group of people who feel one way and then another depending on the day you talk to them!

You'll have to decide for yourself if you want to go the indie route. If you do, take it one step at a time – you don't have to learn every platform, and you don't have to do everything at once. If you're persistent, you will see results (sound familiar?), and you can even look forward to the day when you're big enough to hire help! (Many indie authors get to a point where they outsource things like book covers and social media graphics to assistants).

One other point about going indie: there are lots of *free* resources online about how to master various platforms, how to brand and market yourself, etc. There are lots of inexpensive books on these subjects too. Some of the courses you might see out there on these topics are good value, but *only* after you've exhausted the free material, and *only* after you have gotten a feel for who the trusted course providers are. There are a lot of promise-the-moon courses out there that are just repackaged free stuff, priced outrageously. Buyer beware.

WHAT? IS THIS THE END?

Yes, it's true. The time has come for you to reach out and thwap someone on the funny bone.

Your homework?

1. Take those pieces you've worked up, choose your markets and sell 'em. Send me an incoherent but ecstatic email when you make your first sale.
2. If you liked this book, leave a review online where you bought it.
3. If you would like to get regular blog posts by me, you can sign up here.

ABOUT THE AUTHOR

Chandra Clarke wears many hats, sometimes all at once, which makes it hard to get through doorways. A recovering/relapsing entrepreneur, she will also admit to having been a freelance writer, with publishing credits in places like *Popular Science, Canadian Business* magazines, and yes, *Voice of the Kent Farmer*. These days she likes to write hard science fiction, near future science fiction, humorous fantasy, and nonfiction. If credentials are your thing, she has a PhD in creative writing. Chandra is married to Terry Johnson, the best British import since the Aston Martin, and she's a mother to four kids and two dogs. She thinks they're all pretty awesome, but she might be biased.

http://www.chandrakclarke.com/

www.ingramcontent.com/pod-product-compliance
Lightning Source LLC
Chambersburg PA
CBHW021128080526
44587CB00012B/1187